This book explores the thoughts, opinions, and feelings of the author herself. She writes topics that relate to most of us in our life. The conversation that she has with her own-self provide much comfort to her to find values in the meaning of life.

Nazlina Mirsultan

CONVERSATION WITH MYSELF

AUSTIN MACAULEY PUBLISHERS™

LONDON · CAMBRIDGE · NEW YORK · SHARJAH

A CIP catalogue record for this title is available from the British Library.

ISBN 9781035832149 (Paperback)
ISBN 9781035832156 (Hardback)
ISBN 9781035832163 (ePub e-book)

www.austinmacauley.com

First Published 2024
Austin Macauley Publishers Ltd®
1 Canada Square
Canary Wharf
London
E14 5AA

Table of Contents

Opening Note

It has been for some time now that I wanted to write a book. I am not a professionally trained writer, nor am I a language teacher. English is not even my first language; it is the third language to me. I do not have a solid background to be a potential writer. I began to fall in love with writing during my postgraduate studies. I do read, and reading books is one of my favourite hobbies, besides cooking and gardening.

As a lecturer of twenty years in a college, I believe very strongly in the power of education. It is the ultimate key to achieving success in anything we do in our life. You educate the nation, and you build a better world. I came from a very humble poverty background and had to strive with many challenges to be where I am today; it was a journey worth travelling.

No one really motivated me to start writing; I just felt like noting down my own thoughts. This book is the result of some collections and compilations of my own thoughts, which may differ from others' thoughts. It is good to get to know others' thoughts rather than just your own. It is a part of learning to develop better humans, as the journey of learning never ends.

Let Me Start

I have this habit of talking to myself all the time; it is like my imaginary friend that is always with me. I know that people do talk to themselves; it is something that everyone does. Maybe I talk more to myself than normal people do. I just find comfort in the act that has become like a ritual to me. Do I have a psychological problem? Maybe, to some extent, but then again, what is the definition of normal that we all can agree on without any doubts?

The thing is, at times I do enjoy talking to myself rather than talking to another human being. It gives me comfort in the confidential and private conversation that I have with myself. I do enjoy the company of people, being with friends and family, but conversation with oneself is so deep and sincere. You do not have to speak aloud as it is communicated in silence within you. You can communicate at any time, anywhere, about anything or anyone that you want to; see, it is really your choice. There is no limit on the topic of your conversation, which is fantastic.

Does that mean that I am lonely, that is why I have this habit of talking to myself? Well, part of it is true. Loneliness makes me closer to myself and that is why I converse with myself. I get to understand myself better and learn the deep thoughts and emotions that are in me. Loneliness can be good if you know how to manage it well. Loneliness makes you appreciate the people in your life more; you will appreciate your family, friends, colleagues, and even a stranger.

All those thoughts that you have in your mind, you just go through them one by one, and analyse the ones that you feel are important. It is amazing how you can converse with yourself and at the same time communicate with other people around you. I wonder, can anyone really read your thoughts? Some people sense your thoughts and respond to it. Why is it that some can sense you and others cannot? Does it make any difference to humans? I like to believe it does because I feel so.

When I am with some people that I do not feel very comfortable with, I tell myself to find the exit way immediately. Some people react in this manner in times of need; they give excuses to escape their way. It is not something that your logical mind would be able to accept well. Your logical mind would ask you to provide information on why you are not comfortable, to process those reasons and act accordingly. At times, we know that there is no logic to what we are doing in our lives, but we still prefer to do it. You just can't really explain why you do it. There will not be logic to everything in this life. If we apply the theory of logic to all our actions, there would be many opportunities we would miss out on in life. The standard acceptance of logic itself to each person may not be the same. What may be logically acceptable to me may not be to you; therefore, we find it very difficult to understand the concept of logic itself in life.

1. Stress

Stress is the utmost concern in life today. We live in a world that is full of stress daily. Stress from the responsibilities of work, relationships with family and friends, and the expectations of our society towards us. It has become impossible for one to live without any stress today. The level of stress just seems to keep increasing each day and it occupies space in each of us. Due to this, there is a tremendous increase in illness and diseases, and more importantly, the increase of mental health issues such as depression.

It has become very vital to manage stress today, and people need to learn how to manage it. The need to de-stress yourself from time to time is very much required to enable you to continue living a healthy life. Failure to do so brings a lot of damage to a person in terms of health, relationships, happiness, and success.

We live a stressful life where we find it very hard and rare to experience happiness and contentment. Most people today forget to smile and are always angry at something or someone for some matter. We get upset and jealous when we see someone else happy and enjoying life, which adds to our stress. We question their happiness because we are living a miserable life and we want to see others living a miserable life too.

We want to believe that the stress we are facing currently will end and that it is temporary. In reality, upon the end or even before the end of one problem, there is already another problem to deal with. We must learn how to deal with more than just one problem in life. As long as we live, we will have problems in life, and we need to learn to manage them. The problems do not end; they never will.

2. The Rain

When it rains, the temperature becomes cooler, creating a cosier mood in the environment. Sitting here in my house, watching the raindrops outside my balcony, gives me a wonderful feeling of comfort. Water falling from the sky, drop by drop until it reaches the ground. It makes sounds that become very soothing music to my ears. There is the sound of thunder striking once in a while, and later on, the rain slows down until it completely stops.

The rain does show its anger too when it strikes with thunderstorms and strong blows of wind that come from its direction. Doors and windows shut down violently with a loud noise of a bang. Leaves and branches of trees dance away in the rain according to its rhythm, and cats hide under a table in fear of its sound.

I very much enjoy a cup of tea when it rains. By just watching the rain and feeling the cool breeze that it brings, is my idea of relaxation and meditation. I am one of those people that simply love the rain. Why? I do not know, but I just love it very much. Some people do not like it when it rains; I know some of my friends do not like it. They start to complain and blame the weather for not being able to do what they want. They blame the rain for coming. Sadly, they do not realise that rain brings a lot of blessings to nature, humans, and animals. In some countries, they pray for the rain to fall as they depend on it very much to fulfil their basic needs in life.

I remember when I was a child, playing in the rain outside my house and singing along with the rain song. Those days were the happy moments in my life that I captured eternally. Sometimes I do wish I could play in the rain like how I used to when I was a little girl. Life at that time seemed to be very free of worries. Why could I not enjoy the pleasure of nature now like how I used to? Just go play in the rain when it is raining.

3. Your Favourite Colour

Do you have a favourite colour? What is your favourite colour? When someone asks me that question, I do not answer immediately because I love all colours. Why can't I love all colours? Why do I have to love only one or a few colours? There are so many colours available, and I don't even know all the names of those colours. A colour has many different shades, and with each shade, whether lighter or darker, it becomes a new colour with a different name. When you mix two colours together, they totally become a new colour. So, how can I just give attention to only some colours when there are so many colours that I could explore out there?

Of course, colours do relate to some significant meanings. When you are attending a funeral, the preferred colour you usually wear is black. The bride usually wears a white wedding gown to resemble the purity of the event. People relate to colours throughout their life with events, functions, activities, and so on.

Your mood does relate to the choices of colours you pick. When you are happy, you tend to relate to brighter colours like yellow, orange, or red. When you are feeling down and sad, you tend to relate to darker tones of colours like black and grey. It is amazing how moods can dictate the choice of our colours.

Humans are labelled according to their skin colours such as whites, blacks, browns, yellows, etc. The skin of white people is not the colour of white anyway, and black people are not exactly the colour of black. What is my colour? I am not white, black, or brown. I am just human, blessed with the right skin colour for me. I did not know skin colour could be such an issue when I was a child, but as I grew up, I realised it is. The thought of human beings being labelled with colour really is a mind disease that needs to end. It has been happening for far too long now; how much longer does this need to go on? When is this going to end?

Can you imagine your life in black and white? We need colours in life as we all have feelings, and you can't separate feelings from life. Life and colours are inseparable.

4. When Is the Right Time

There are things we do in our life that make us feel the need to find the right time to do them. The question is, when is the right time? It's always something we ponder. Sometimes we just wait for the right time to come in our life, but sometimes it just does not seem to be coming. Should we wait for the right time before we start doing something, or should we just do it right away when we have the time and opportunity at hand? Which is the right answer, and why?

At times, we want to reserve the task for the right time, and we tend to find excuses for procrastinating until we feel it is the right time. This practice can become a habit, and we blame it on the situations we were in for not being able to have the right time to proceed with that particular task. We do feel good for having valid reasons for not accomplishing the task, and as long as we have something to blame it on for not doing it, it is alright.

Those who do not wait for the right time and just do it may face a risk of not getting the desired results. That is also something we would give as a reason for not achieving the best of what we expect it to be. This action is carried out by people without a proper plan and unprepared in carrying out the task. Let us just do it and see what happens, rather than wait and see what happens.

Nevertheless, some people hold the opinion that there is a time for everything and when you do things at the wrong time, you may create a disaster. So, should we wait for the right time to do it, or just do it right away when we want to do it? What should it be?

Only time can tell when the best time for anything to happen or to be done. Time is such a mystery for us to understand and it will continue remaining a mystery until the end of time. Time waits for no man, and no man can control time. The amazing thing is that time never stops ticking; it continues to tick forward, tick, tick, tick.

5. Pain

I wonder how our body registers pain. How much of a pain reception does our body respond to, be it mild or severe? The brain relates to everything in our body, including pain. Sometimes I wonder how it can be possible that pain is detected and sensed from our brain, but the wound, cut, or fracture is in other parts of our body. The brain is not injured; instead, the sensory is activated from the brain first before it travels to the injury. We feel the pain only at the injured part and not at our brain; there is a connection between the brain and the injury.

Does emotional pain relate to physical pain? When a person is emotionally hurt, why does it cause so much pain in your heart, while the whole body just seems to be stiff, heavy, and inflamed? When we are sad or depressed, we experience pain in our heart, a sharp pain as if you are being stabbed deep inside. Our heart is bleeding and crying with us when we are sad. The pain stops when we are no longer sad or depressed; this indicates that emotional pain can trigger physical pain.

Does emotional pain lead to illness? In fact, it does; many studies have proven this theory. I do believe it is one of the main contributors to illness. Human emotions are very fragile and a significant element to our body and life. Everything we do relates to our emotions because emotions create meaning in our life.

It is very true when people say, "Take care of your heart," because you will have a much healthier and longer life.

6. Relationship

We naturally develop relationships with everything or everyone around us. For instance, the weather; we all have a relationship with it. When it is sunny and bright, we usually feel much cheerier and happier. During winter or autumn, more people experience depression and sadness, thus the rate of suicide increases during this season.

I feel at ease and very peaceful sitting under a tree, and when the wind blows on my face and passes me by, it is such a joy. I talk to trees, and I strongly feel the trees listen to what I say and understand it too; they can feel you and sense you very well. I personally feel that I can relate better to animals rather than humans because animals are simply pure, unlike humans who often have their hidden agendas. Truly, animals are very loving creatures, we can learn a lot from them, especially about relationships. Their understanding of relationships is much greater compared to us humans. I just cannot imagine this world without the animal kingdom. The truth is we need them more than they need us.

Today, we do not just have relationships with living creatures, but we also relate to non-living objects. All the gadgets we use in our lives, such as laptops and mobile phones, we use daily for hours. Without them, we are unable to function well in life; we become too dependent on them for most of our tasks. These gadgets have become our needs in life; without them, it has become impossible to carry out our responsibilities. The assurance that humans will create more new gadgets to be used in the future is definite.

Relationships between humans are at stake nowadays; people tend to spend less time together. More people are willing to be alone and spend time with their gadgets rather than with real humans. The lack of quality in human relationships today is due to the modern lifestyle, and this is one of the main reasons for the increase in mental health issues.

At times, you feel that no one really cares about you or wants to know how you are coping in life. Everybody seems to be just too busy for you; it makes you feel that everything else is more important than you are. This might be true because they admit to you that they were busy with work, studies, or whatever things are going on in their life.

When your loved ones are with you today, make time for them. You need to put them as your priority in life, put effort and do your best to make them happy. The majority of us tend to realise their existence only upon their departure.

7. Arguments

During arguments, we usually shout at each other and use words that are very harsh with the intention of hurting the other party. At that moment, we do not consider or care much about others' feelings; our only concern, which is very important, is that we need to win the argument. However, later, when you are much calmer, you regret what you have said earlier during the argument. By now, it is too late to retract what you have already said aloud. One disadvantage of the communication process is that whatever has been said cannot be erased or retracted; there is no rewind or edit button to change it later. It is already out there, known, read, and heard by people.

Of course, you could apologise for whatever you have said, and chances are you may be pardoned and forgiven, but this is not guaranteed. Even though you were forgiven, the situation may not be the same any longer as it used to be. Some will still remember what you said and how hurtful it may still be for a very long time; it may even be forever. For some people, the incident may have happened several years ago, but it just feels like yesterday, very fresh in their mind. That argument has left a tremendous impact on their life; they are no longer the same person they used to be before.

Some arguments may lead to physical fights, which could cause physical injury, and this may leave scars or marks on the body as evidence. It is even harder to forget the incident because every time you look at those scars or marks, it reminds you of the very incident. The presence of both physical and emotional harm is much greater in memory.

We humans will have arguments; it is a part of our nature and survival instinct. It is impossible to avoid them in our life, but how we manage them is more crucial. It can build you or break you; there is good and bad to it.

8. Your Neighbours

You are considered very lucky if your neighbours are good citizens; otherwise, you are unlucky. Some people do not place much importance on who their neighbours are because they simply mind their own business. They live in their own bubble, ignorant of their surroundings. While some people are rarely at home due to work, leaving early in the morning and returning late at night, they probably have never met their neighbours due to the odd hours they keep.

I remember some of the neighbours we had; most of them were helpful and friendly. As a child, I remember playing with my neighbours' sons or daughters, which was a cherished memory. We would cycle around the neighbourhood together and play outdoor games. My siblings and their siblings became friends as we grew up together; we even went to the same schools. It was normal for us to visit each other's houses to play, eat, or just hang out. We became close with their family members too. Their parents looked out for us just as they did for their own children; it felt like one big happy family. Despite coming from different ethnic groups and religions, this did not stop us from bonding; in fact, it taught us to value each other more. During festive seasons, we celebrated each other's festivals together; we would invite them, and they would invite us to join in the celebrations. Years passed, and then we moved to a new neighbourhood and made new friends.

Remembering those times makes me happy. My siblings and I had good friends and enjoyable times during our childhood, thanks to our neighbours. We are all grown up now and each of us has gone our separate ways, with only a few of us still in touch. Sometimes, I wonder what happened to them, where they are now, and what they are doing in life. I hope they are all doing well.

9. Waiting

Waiting is not an activity that anyone would be keen on doing, especially when it involves a long period. Whether waiting for a bus, test results, a response or feedback from someone, the experience is rarely enjoyable. The waiting period can feel interminably long, as if time has stopped. I remember waiting for my biopsy result for a few days; those days seemed endless.

During your wait, you harbour hopes, desires, goals, and expectations. Sometimes, you are willing to wait longer if the anticipated outcome is positive and fulfils your expectations. This kind of waiting is worthwhile because it meets your hopes. Unfortunately, not all waits result in positive outcomes. Sometimes, the results can be frustrating, painful, and difficult to accept.

How our minds accept the results of our waiting is crucial. When we have waited a long time with a certain expectation, comprehending a different reality can be challenging if the result does not align with our expectations. Sometimes, waiting becomes habitual, as if we have been waiting all our lives and fear the end due to potential disappointment. We find comfort in the act of waiting itself because it signifies that the end has not yet come.

Often, people advise us to wait for the right time, the right person to love, or the right opportunity. We find ourselves continually waiting for what we assume to be the right thing. Most of us have this habit of waiting for something in our lives; we are always waiting for something to happen. The wait goes on and on, and the 'something' may never happen because we are still waiting.

10. Mood Swings

Today, my mood is simply to relax and pamper myself. It has been raining since last night, and it rained the entire day today. The coldness brought by the rain is comforting for a day of staying at home. Sitting on my sofa with a great book to read and tea by my side seems such a great pleasure.

Our mood changes from time to time according to our feelings, the state of emotion we are in, and our environment. I acknowledge that in hot and humid weather, I get agitated and angry more easily. However, in cool and breezy weather, I am much more relaxed and calmer. I don't know the specific reasons, but that's just how it is with me.

Of course, the people you are with are also a major factor affecting your mood. For instance, you could be very jolly and happy, but in just a second, someone can upset you with what they say or do.

At times, I suddenly have the mood to eat something or bake a cake, and I will be very motivated to do it. This mood seems to appear out of nowhere. I do wonder why, but it just happens that way sometimes. When your mood is not good, you are not able to work properly, and the result is usually not so good. Conversely, great results come when you are in a good mood.

When I wake up in the morning, some days my mood starts off very well and other days, it's just very bad. Our mood in the morning is especially important as it influences the rest of the day. Some mornings, I feel good, positive, and energetic. On some days, I just don't feel like waking up at all. I wish I could just continue sleeping. The thought of going through another day already makes me feel exhausted and tired of life itself. Thinking of going through the cycle of each day again and again, I ask myself what the purpose of my existence and life is.

Humans tend to display the mood they are experiencing through their facial expressions, posture, movements, and reactions to what they are dealing with in life. A sincere smile that you give can really affect the people around you. The good mood you carry can spread good vibes to others around you. Unfortunately, you can also spread negative vibes, and it is contagious.

11. Must Love Cats

Cats are very magnificent creatures. I have two cats, namely Golmol and Millie. They are my best buddies and life comforters. I talk to them about my daily matters; they are great listeners. The best thing is they never argue with you; all they say is 'meow meow meow' as feedback.

Cats are very loving creatures, and I have learned a lot from my cats. We humans are much more complicated compared to cats or any other animals. Animals are pure and do not have any hidden agendas towards you. That is why I trust animals much more than humans.

Their love is unconditional. Cats can sense your feelings; when I am sad and feeling very down, my cats detect that signal very well. They try to cheer me up and sit close to me; their warmth really makes my day much better. I can feel their affection, love, and concern.

Cats are one of the cleanest animals on earth; they groom themselves more than other animals. I bathe my cats and take them to the vet for regular check-ups, jabs, and treatment. That is the responsibility you need to carry when you have them as your pets; otherwise, do not keep them as pets. Just because they do not have a voice does not make it right for you to treat them however you want. You need to treat them fairly and kindly; it is an investment you will never regret in your life. They give you so much love and affection that takes away all your worries and stress, truly a medication to your soul.

After a hard day of work, I just want to go back home to my Golmol and Millie. They wait for my arrival at the door, and once I unlock it, they run towards me so that I can pat and hold them. They follow me everywhere – to the room, kitchen, and even the bathroom. They demand attention and affection. Once they have settled down, I make my tea and sit with them, and we have our chat for the day. I can share everything with them; there are no secrets between my cats and me. They know me better than any human I know.

12. My Teatime

My teatime in the evening is very essential to me. I look forward to my teatime every day, chai (Indian tea), as it is known in my mother tongue. I am very precise about my chai; it must meet my taste standards. Otherwise, I will not drink it – yes, I am very fussy about my tea. I enjoy my chai in a cup each evening, accompanied by some biscuits or cakes. I only have one cup of chai every evening; I do not make a habit of pouring a second cup unless I have visitors with me. I do enjoy having conversations with my visitors during my teatime. I restrict myself from having too many cookies and cakes during teatime because they might spoil my appetite for dinner. I can't fill up my tummy with no space left for dinner.

Originally, my chai time is my quiet moment of the day, a time for myself to let go of all the stress of the day. I sit on the balcony, where I have created a mini garden with many pots of plants, just to escape from the busy hassle of the world outside.

As I sip my chai from the cup, I feel as though the stress is slipping away from my body. My chai is my comforter of the day. The day doesn't feel complete without having my chai; if possible, I do not want to skip my teatime for any reason. Unless, of course, there is something major that cannot be avoided, such as my house being on fire or an earthquake.

Of course, there are many ways of making tea, and my way is the traditional method. I just boil the tea leaves on the stove, add milk to it, and once it has boiled and reached a colour that I approve of, I switch off the stove. I filter it into a cup and add some brown sugar for taste. I only drink the tea while it is still hot. My teatime is also my reflection time for the day; while enjoying my tea, I process some of the incidents that have happened that day.

My teatime is my therapeutic session that I have every evening, which helps to re-energize me to continue with the rest of my day. My teatime is not very long, though; it is about 15 to 30 minutes at most. It's amazing how that short period of time can do wonders for me. How do you enjoy your tea?

13. Trees

I cannot imagine this world without trees. Can you? If you think about it, trees are such an important living element in this world. It fascinates me that trees provide oxygen to us, and that is our very basic necessity for survival. I love sitting under a tree for hours as it really helps to relax my mind from all the turbulence in this hectic and challenging life. If you really take the time to be attentive to the trees around you, amazingly, you will notice that each of them is not identical at all. They are not standardised products but each has its own personality, character, and is unique in its own way. They each have their own brand name. Even the leaves from a tree are not the same. Isn't it wonderful that each of the leaves does not look the same?

Randomly, I do analyse trees standing tall on sunny or rainy days, or be it day or night, they are still standing tall no matter what, and still standing strong. It is not a choice for them to go through all the seasons, and when it is a windy day, you can see their leaves dance away according to the rhythm the wind is blowing.

Some people believe that you should talk to your plants; they will grow well and healthy. I have the habit of talking to my plants, I feel as though they listen and do understand my conversations with them. It is just one of those superstitious things that you cannot prove. I realised that my plants are much healthier when I talk to them. No serious talk, just asking them how they are or talking about the weather and singing a song or two when I water them in the morning. I also try to make time to trim and groom them up once in a while so that they look neat, tidy, and presentable. I have many pots of plants at the front entrance of my house and a lot more at the back in the balcony. I also have some water-based plants in my kitchen and bathroom. They keep me company, and my house feels cooler, greener, and healthier with them. They relax my eyes too as they are beautiful to look at. I enjoy them in my life very much, and my cats love to sit and have their nap on the balcony as it is a very comfortable place between the pots of plants.

14. Food

Food is a basic human need for survival. It is not an option, but a necessity for us humans. In some parts of the world, people are dying each day due to hunger, while in other parts, food is wasted without any sense of guilt. The thought of people dying each day from hunger deeply upsets me. This should not be happening in today's world. Why is it still occurring? I find many people still do not realise how grateful they should be for having food on their table each day.

In the modern world, we consume a lot of processed food, and fewer people are eating real food. These processed foods are full of unhealthy ingredients such as high sugar and saturated fats. No wonder people today are not healthy and are suffering from diseases and illnesses. So many children are obese and have developed health issues at a very young age, while the fertility of men and women is affected too.

The fast-food industry is growing very rapidly, and most households do not cook much nowadays due to a busy lifestyle.

It is often said, "You are what you eat."

15. Disappointment

It is a very heavy feeling, isn't it, when you are disappointed? Indeed, it becomes difficult to trust the person who has disappointed you again with all your heart. If that person frequently disappoints you, it becomes unbearable to cope with it any longer. It eats away at you slowly and affects your behaviour, emotions, and mental health.

There comes a stage where you mentally prepare yourself for more disappointment from that person. The person causing the disappointment thinks it's okay and no big deal to treat you that way. Why is that so? Perhaps it's because we keep accepting it time and again, or perhaps deep down in our hearts, we still harbour hope that this time, we will not be disappointed again by that person. You believe that person will fulfil their promises, not just offering empty words like before. Secretly, you hold onto hope and believe that this time, they will not come up with excuses or reasons to justify their lack of responsibility in delivering on their promises. Ultimately, you reach a stage of realisation that you will always be disappointed by that person, no matter what you do or say.

Yet, this episode will repeat itself over and over until the disappointed person loses hope in the promises made and decides to let go. Perhaps it's just exhaustion from trying to understand or seeking clarification, only to accept the situation because, in the end, it all just becomes part of the past.

16. The Magic of a Smile

Smiling is a very natural act, and it doesn't cost you anything as it is free of charge. If you can make someone happy with your smile, why don't you smile, right?

I do smile; it's a very natural thing to do, but sometimes the response I get is not welcoming. Some people give me a weird look, as if they are asking, "Why is she smiling?" I can immediately sense it. Some people will try to smile back as if they don't have a choice. While others just look at you straight in the eye and choose to ignore you. They walk past you as if you were not there, as if you do not exist. It makes you feel like you are not important and not worth anything in this world.

However, when someone smiles at you from their heart and makes the effort to acknowledge you, instantly you can feel the warmth and love given to you. What a wonderful, pleasant feeling that is.

A lot of people seem to forget that a smile is free of charge, you don't have to pay for it. It is one of the actions that benefit your health very much; it keeps you away from the doctor. The magic of a smile works miraculously for your body, mind, and soul. When someone smiles at me, it just makes my day better. Sadly, in today's world, people don't smile much at each other anymore. They are so occupied with their hectic lives that they forget to smile and acknowledge the importance of this little act in life. Some people associate a smile with weakness, or out of concern for their status quo or social class, they prohibit themselves or their children from smiling at others. My question is, what can you lose by offering a smile to others?

I feel sad for them and the society they have become. Learn to smile, and the world will smile back at you. I still believe in that until today. So just smile, and the magic will begin. Try it!

17. Love

I strongly believe that love conquers all. It is the most natural need in our life. We all need love, and we cannot live life without it. Life would be very lonely, depressing, and painful without love. You can't deny it, because that is true.

Some people seem to have love very easily in their life, while others need to work very hard for it. We love our family, friends, and even our pets. One thing is for sure: in all stages of our life, we need love. Children need their parents' love very much as they depend on them.

Reaching adolescence, you tend to find love in someone special, and if the relationship goes well, you may end up marrying that person. With marriage comes children, and the love you have for your children is endless.

Love is not exclusively for humans only; love for animals and nature is part of our life. Some people are not very lucky in love because it is absent in their life. Children who were abandoned by their parents at birth will always question themselves as to why they were born or abandoned. The rage and hatred can poison their life. The percentage of childbirth out of wedlock is increasing and is becoming common and norm in most countries today. These children are often brought up by a single parent, usually their mother, with the father absent in their life.

Today, women can choose to fertilise their eggs from sperm banks; these men are total strangers whom they have never met or known. Sadly, it has become an accepted practice in our lifestyle. Some people debate on this topic and stand by the women's rights to get pregnant; they believe it is our body, and we have the right over our own body. But what about these children's rights? They did not ask to be brought into this world and grow up without their father's presence in their life. The male donors may end up having many children whom they don't even know of. These children do not know their own siblings and could end up marrying each other in the future. Isn't that incest?

Love is so powerful that people are willing to kill or commit suicide for it. It is not something that you can explain logically to someone; it is something you just need to feel, go through, and experience yourself. When it comes to feelings, the jurisdiction of logic does not apply anymore. When one is deprived of love in life, contentment is no longer present. Negativity will take over, bringing a lot of pain and hurt, which is bad for your health and soul. Anxiety and depression are common behaviours in most people who lack love in their lives, which a lot of people are suffering from nowadays.

Does true love exist? We strive to look for it, and the search continues. Finding true love in humans seems to be impossible because humans will disappoint you at times, no matter how good you are to them. Does that mean that we should stop loving people? Of course not; we need to remember that as humans, we are all not perfect; we have our strengths and weaknesses. Learn to love them anyway, accepting the good and bad of that person. When you love someone, you learn to trust them and accept them with all your heart.

True love comes from our creator; the Lord's love is always unlimited and unconditional. If you do not believe in God, you should know that God still loves you.

18. Family

When I was young, I always thought that I came from my mother's tummy, and all my siblings too came from the same tummy. I thought it must be a magical tummy because it could produce us; of course, I laugh about it now, knowing the truth about the facts of life.

Sometimes, I wonder why I was born into this family, as it isn't something that I could choose. We cannot choose our parents, siblings, or our maternal and paternal family members. Blood relations are a bond that has been connected to us before we even exist in this world; it is a connection that we cannot deny.

Family is important, as they are the first people we get to know when growing up. The role of parents is very important, and their responsibility is to take care of and guide us; with this, they shape and mould our behaviour. Some people are lucky to have a loving and caring family, thus their bonding is very strong with each other. Not all of us are lucky enough to have that happiness in life. Some people are orphans and have no family members; it isn't something that they choose, but it is just what it is.

The mother is the one who keeps the family members connected and bonding close together. She always thinks about her children first above anything else. The role of a father is to provide and support the family, as he is the man of the house. Every family has problems they need to manage and overcome. Arguments, misunderstandings, and conflicts naturally happen. There are stories in each family, and no matter what happens, they are still family, and nothing can change that. At times, you may not have spoken to some of your family members for a long time, which could be years. Somehow, you will speak to this person again and form a stronger connection with them. You will always be related to each other as you are blood-related; you cannot change that, no matter what.

19. God

Do you believe in God? The Lord that created us, the sun, the moon, the sky, the mountains, the ocean, trees, animals, and everything?

I believe that God exists with all my heart. God exists, and we cannot see Him in a physical form; we can only see Him emotionally and spiritually when we believe in Him with all our hearts. The matter of God is beyond our understanding, and we cannot comprehend Him because we are one of His creations, while He is the Creator.

Some people try to understand the existence and purpose of life with logic, which contributes to a new creation of faith and religion. It is not the teaching of God, but humans trying to play God. This new faith and religion have their own values and philosophy, which is unclear in seeking the truth.

We all are not immortal; the moment we were born, one thing that is confirmed is our death. No one can escape death, not even the rich and powerful. When you are dead, your physical body ceases, but your soul returns to God, to your owner eternally.

This world is just a temporary stop, a journey of many trials that we all need to go through, and the results of our behaviour will be analysed in the hereafter. Whether you did good or bad in your life journey, you will be given appropriate rewards or punishments accordingly. That is the promise of God the Almighty.

God knows better than we do, as what we know is very little. People who do not believe in God will regret their actions on the day of the final judgement. How can you not accept your creator? Without God, you would not even exist!

Think about it.

20. Wind

The wind is something that we cannot see but can feel. It blows in all directions, sometimes slowly and at other times, very strongly. We can enjoy a mild and moderate blow of the wind but not a strong one, as it can destroy us and change our landscapes. A tornado can destroy everything on land.

I always wonder, where does this wind come from? Why is it slow at times and very strong at others? Who controls it? It is unseen, but we feel it, so we acknowledge the existence of the wind. This proves to us that just because something is unseen does not mean it does not exist.

I enjoy the wind very much. On a windy day, I love to sit on a swing under a tree and enjoy the wind blowing through me. That is such a joy and a very relaxing moment. I observe the trees dancing in the rhythm of the wind, a beautiful moment to capture.

At those moments, your mind may drift somewhere, perhaps thinking of someone whom you love and miss. The wind can take your mind to places and moments that are precious to you. Your mind blows wherever the wind takes you.

21. Friendship

We choose our friends, as the elderly say, "Choose your friends wisely." Why? Because they significantly influence our lives. Growing up in a multi-racial country, Malaysia, my friends come from different ethnicities. Some of my friends are Malay; some are Chinese, while others are Indians. It's great because I learn a lot of things from them, such as their culture and traditions. I enjoy their food and have since learned to cook them myself. Who doesn't like eating delicious food, right?

They also taught me some important words in their vocabulary. I remember spending good times with them while growing up. Some of my friends are doing very well in their lives with good jobs and happy family lives. However, not all are lucky; some of them are not doing so well either at work or with family. Very few of us are keeping in touch; most of the others are out of touch. Gone with the wind and unknown as to what happened to them. Probably they go where life takes them, continuing their journey in their own way. Well, that happens, and we learn to accept it as part of our life journey.

Friends you have when you are children are somehow much more special compared to friends you have in your adult life cycle. As children, you are very naïve and innocent; you don't judge your friends. There's no discrimination or bias; everything seems to be well in friendship. Children have very pure hearts and therefore are truthful in friendship. Unfortunately, as you grow up, those important values start to slowly diminish and become less important. Some people are friends because they expect something from you. Friendship starts to have a different meaning altogether by now. It is no longer about wanting to share time together through thick and thin. It is more about taking advantage of each other for one's own self-interests. You may have doubts about your friends; are they trustworthy? Sometimes you hide the reality from them so that you can still be their friend.

I have learned that sometimes it is much better not to share all the information with your friends, as some may backstab you and hurt you for their own agenda. "Whom can I trust?" That is the question that you ask yourself, and the answer may not be available immediately but may come to you in time.

Good friends are hard to find. When you have found them in your life, learn to appreciate them; they are friends for life. These are friends that you can rely on as they will be there in times of need. They can sense when you are feeling despair and sadness and be there for you to help and support you through those difficult and painful moments in life. They try to ease the pain for you by being present in your life. Not everyone is lucky enough to have good friends in their life. I am happy to say that I do have these friends in my life; they make my life feel much more meaningful and beautiful for me. Thanks to them for being a part of my journey in this life. To my friends, I am sending you all lots of love.

22. Marriage

Every girl dreams of a prince charming to marry one day. A prince as a husband is what we girls always fantasise about in our little imaginary world. As a little girl, the fantasy of a charming prince was very real and exciting. However, as you grow up, these dreams seem to slowly fade away. What happened? You woke up from your sleep and realised the real world is not like the one in your dreams.

The little girl is no longer little; she has now become a woman. She is learning about the reality of men in the real world. As she gets to know men better, the charm she once felt is slowly diminishing. Sadly, she realises that there are very few good men left in the real world.

She will marry the one with whom she is content, not necessarily one she loves. She doesn't have to really love him, as she finds that love is no longer the utmost priority in a marriage. For her, as long as he is responsible and loyal, he is good enough to fill the position of a husband. She has learned one important thing: to compromise with love.

Most women today decide to marry men who can assure them a comfortable life and material possessions. Very few marry for love nowadays; women are becoming much more practical in life, analysing their future husbands in terms of materialistic needs rather than seeking love itself.

Marriage failures are common in this modern world, and the divorce rate has increased rapidly in society. Children are the ones most affected by marriage failures, suffering emotional pain and going through breakdowns and prolonged depression. No wonder the rate of depression and mental health issues has increased tremendously among children at a very early age.

Divorce is an ugly process. Parents may fight for custody and ask their children to choose whom they want to be with, either their mother or father. This causes great stress on the children as they do not want to hurt either parent. The parents may move on with their lives, some finding new partners and remarrying. This new person may not be welcomed by their children; to them, he or she will always be a stranger in the family.

The distance between the parents and their children starts to become much more obvious. Some parents do not give importance to this feeling, their child will learn to accept this next person as they spend more time together and get to know each other better. The child's needs have become unnoticed. Some of the major reasons for marriage failure are a lack of trust and not being responsible.

Some couples still stay in their marriage, although they are no longer happy together. The number one reason is for the sake of their children. The children are completely aware of the unhappy marriage between their parents. They are emotionally affected, and their perceptions of marriage are influenced by their parents' behaviour. This is an unhappy family stuck together.

Partners do not want to acknowledge that their marriage has ended and are willing to struggle and try to prolong it for the sake of their children. How can you make others happy when you are not happy yourself?

The majority of elderly divorced women with children usually do not remarry. They feel their life is at a different stage; the longing for physical affection from a man is no longer important. They can live without it and still find happiness in their own way. They are content with their lives surrounded by their children, family, friends, and pets. Their time is occupied with house chores, family, and friends. They can survive as a single parent. Some of my friends are single parents and they seem much happier now than before. Although at times they admit to feeling lonely for companionship, someone to talk to and share their life with, otherwise they manage their life just fine on their own.

However, it is a different story with men; they do not seem to cope very well being a single parent or being on their own without a partner. The majority of men will find a new partner to fill that void in their life. Their main reason is to fulfil their physical needs. They are not able to cope well on their own. It is very rare to find men who can go on with their life well on their own after their divorce. In this sense, women are emotionally much stronger compared to men.

23. Boss

As a career woman, I have worked with many superiors as my bosses. Throughout my 20 years of work experience, I have learned that the toughest affair at work is the relationship with people in the workplace. Most people leave their job because they do not get along well with others at the workplace. That is the number one reason why people leave their job, topping the list with the highest percentage. Other reasons are an inability to cope well with the job, dissatisfaction with the job, health issues, and family responsibilities and matters.

Your boss is important because he/she conducts the appraisals that determine your work performance. At the end of the day, it is his/her words that count, not yours. The kind of personality and behaviour your boss has is shown in the manner of how people are treated at the workplace. Therefore, it is very important to have a good understanding with your boss. The thing is, you need to understand your boss; it is not so important for your boss to understand you, but it is much more important for you to understand your boss if you want to progress in your job.

At times, you may disagree with your boss on certain decisions made or approaches used, but at the end of the day, it is still your boss who makes the final decision. The reality is that bosses do feel insecure about their position among competent subordinates who can outperform them. They are afraid of losing their position to these subordinates. That's why they downplay the performance of these subordinates to secure their position in the organisation. That is one of the reasons why your boss does not teach you everything you need to know; you must learn it yourself. Why should they? It took them many years of work to learn and be where they are today. This is one of the techniques used by the majority of bosses to secure their position in the organisation, especially the senior bosses who have been in the organisation for many years.

Certain subordinates become immune to their boss's behaviour and learn to just accept it as part of their working life. New subordinates may be very motivated with their job and have high hopes towards their boss. However, after some time, the same motivation and hope they had at the beginning of their career seem to slowly fade away.

Some bosses with effective leadership skills usually do not stay very long in their current position, as they are eager to grow and develop their skills in many other fields of interest. Those who tend to stay too long in their position are the ones who become very comfortable with their authority and power. Overall, these bosses have the tendency to influence the organisation's values and long-term goals. Due to their long service in the organisation, they play a major part in influencing the work culture and philosophy of the organisation.

Male or female boss, which one is better? Which gender is your choice for a better boss? It is true that female bosses are more emotional compared to male bosses, with some advantages and disadvantages to this. Being too emotional on a matter could be a good thing or a bad thing. A strong positive emotion builds your strength, while a negative emotion is your weakness as it brings you down. Male bosses are more neutral in their emotional stability compared to female bosses; with emotional stability, it helps to contribute to professional behaviour at work. However, at times, subordinates may require and expect their male bosses to display more emotional responses, such as caring more and having empathy towards them. Both genders, be it male or female, have their own advantages and disadvantages as bosses.

24. Health

The best gift for someone is good health. Many of us do not realise the importance of being healthy until we have suffered from any kind of illness. Illness makes you appreciate your health, and you pray to get well soon and to be healthy again.

During illness, we suffer from pain; some pain is tolerable, while some is tremendously excruciating and unbearable. When you are going through this worst pain, which you cannot bear and tolerate, you wish to die so that the pain just stops. When you are suffering from the pain, the only thing you think of is how to make the pain stop, and there is nothing else in your mind. You will be amazed at what pain can make you do.

Personally, I have experienced this worst pain myself. I was diagnosed with breast cancer a few years back, it was metastasis cancer at stage 3, a very fast-spreading cancer that had spread to my lymph nodes. The treatment plan was explained to me by my doctor; however, there was no guarantee of my surviving the cancer. I remember very clearly that I told my doctor, no one could guarantee my survival except God. I would do whatever I could to treat myself and leave the rest to God. The next day I started my chemotherapy and my journey to fight the disease began. It took me 6 months to complete all the required treatments, which included chemotherapy, surgery, and radiotherapy. I completed my treatment much earlier because usually, it takes nine months to one and a half years to treat breast cancer. Compared to other types of cancer, breast cancer has a higher survival rate. The experience taught me many things in life; my perspective on life is now renewed. You will only truly understand it when you experience it yourself; otherwise, you will not know the real essence of it. Even though I was facing many challenges and had complaints about what was going on in my life at that time, I still wanted to live and was not ready to die. I prayed that God would give me another chance at life so that I would be kinder to life.

Scientists and doctors believe that pain is sensed in our brain first before it travels to other parts of our body where it is injured. Therefore, they believe that by manipulating our brain we could lessen the sensation of the pain.

The human body is so amazing to analyse because in trying to understand our body better and to discover more knowledge, many studies are being conducted. Pharmaceutical companies have invented and created many medicines to cure illnesses. A variety of supplements are being commercialised and made available for us to consume with the promise of making us healthier and stronger. The thing is, do we need all these supplements, and do they really make us healthier, or do they cause more harm to our body?

Living in a modern lifestyle today, we need to supplement our body. We are living a hectic life, always busy and rushing somewhere; we could not have a complete nutrient diet for our body. These supplements can help us in providing the nutrients to our diet. However, you cannot just rely on supplements to build a healthy body; you need to take care of your lifestyle. Some of the supplements may cause side effects to your body. This is a lesson learned for me in purchasing supplements for my body.

25. Time

Why is a day 24 hours? How did we humans time that so accurately? We have seconds, minutes, and hours in our life. Does time get shorter each day? A day seemed to go by much longer at the beginning of time as compared to nowadays. Time seems to just pass us by so fast; life seems to be at a speed nowadays.

We always find ourselves rushing through our daily tasks and activities, chasing time to ensure that we can complete those tasks before the end of the day. It is so exhausting to move at a fast-track motion and always chasing something to be done. Naturally, it contributes to a very stressful life, always in fast-forward actions.

In today's world, everyone is always rushing into everything, and we have no time to spare for things that are not a priority in our life. What is a priority to most people in this modern world is to work towards earning more money, and that is why people work long hours. They spend most of their time at work, with no time for other things in life, as we are living in a materialistic world today. Time is money, that is what the business world has taught us, and it is very much true.

We always seem to forget that time is a gift; it is not going to be available to us forever and ever. Most of us do not realise the value of time until we have an incident that reminds us of this reality, that we have limited time in our life to be here.

Sometimes we wish we could rewind back the time to correct our mistakes in the past so that we do not have regrets in our present life, as we all want to feel good about ourselves. Unfortunately, that is something impossible, as we cannot travel back in time. Time does not permit us to control it, but it does allow us to manage it, and how we manage our time is entirely up to us.

Everything happens at the right time. When you think of it, you will realise that if it did not happen at those times, a lot of other things would not have happened too, the good times and the bad times.

I have learned a lot from time; it teaches me more each day. The older you grow, the wiser you become. Time tells us that there is a starting point and an ending point. Everything that starts will end, and nothing is permanent; it is all a matter of time. How much time you have, you will never know; only time can tell.